KLAROGO

WHITE══════BOOK

KLORAN

Knights of the Ku Klux Klan

K - U N O
KARACTER
HONOR DUTY

Imperial Palace
KNIGHTS OF THE KU KLUX KLAN
Atlanta, Ga.

FIFTH EDITION

COPYRIGHT 1916
BY W. J. SIMMONS
ATLANTA, GA:

KLORAN

Knights
of the
Ku Klux
Klan

—CAUTION—

PRINTED BY THE KU KLUX PRESS

The
Ku Klux Kreed

WE, the Order of the Knights of the Ku Klux Klan, reverentially acknowledge the majesty and supremacy of the Divine Being, and recognize the goodness and providence of the same.

WE recognize our relation to the government of the United States of America, the supremacy of its Constitution, the Union of States thereunder, and the Constitutional Laws thereof, and we shall be ever devoted to the sublime principles of a pure Americanism and valiant in the defense of its ideals and institutions.

WE avow the distinction between the races of mankind as same has been decreed by the Creator, and we shall ever be true in the faithful maintenance of White Supremacy and will strenuously oppose any compromise thereof in any and all things.

WE appreciate the intrinsic value of a real practical fraternal relationship among men of kindred thought, purpose and ideals and the infinite benefits accruable therefrom, and we shall faithfully devote ourselves to the practice of an honorable Clanishness that the life and living of each may be a constant blessing to others.

"NON SILBA SED ANTHAR"
—Original Creed Revised.

KNIGHTS OF THE KU KLUX KLAN

ORDER OF BUSINESS

1. OPENING CEREMONY.
2. READING OF APPROVED MINUTES.
3. READING OF UNAPPROVED MINUTES OR AMENDMENTS.
4. APPLICATIONS FOR CITIZENSHIP.
5. RECOMMENDATIONS.
6. CEREMONY OF NATURALIZATION.
7. DOES ANY KLANSMAN KNOW OF A KLANSMAN OR A KLANSMAN'S FAMILY WHO IS IN NEED OF FINANCIAL OR FRATERNAL ASSISTANCE?
8. REPORT OF STANDING OR SPECIAL COMMITTEES.
9. BILLS AND COMMUNICATIONS.
10. UNFINISHED BUSINESS.
11. GENERAL BUSINESS.
12. ANNOUNCEMENTS.
13. ELECTION AND INSTALLATION OF OFFICERS.
14. FOR THE ENCOURAGEMENT AND EDIFICATION OF THE KLAN.
15. PAYMENT OF KLAN DUES OR OTHER INDEBTEDNESS TO THE KLAN.
16. KLIGRAPP'S STATEMENT OF RECEIPTS AND DISBURSEMENTS AND THEIR BALANCES.
17. READING AND APPROVING OF MINUTES.
18. CLOSING CEREMONY.

LIST OF KLAN OFFICERS WITH
EXPLANATION OF TITLES.

Exalted Cyclops_____(President)

Klaliff_____(Vice-President)

Klokard_____(Lecturer)

Kludd_____(Chaplain)

Kligrapp_____(Secretary)

Klabee_____(Treasurer)

Kladd_____(Conductor)

Klarogo_____(Inner Guard)

Klexter_____(Outer Guard)

Klokan (singular)_____(Investigator)

Klokann (plural)_____(Board of Investigators)

Night-Hawk_____(Chg. Candidates)

The first four named are station officers.
The Night-Hawk is purely a kloranic officer.

4

IMPERIAL DECREE

Series 1, No. 4.

SUBJECT—THE KLORAN.

TO — EXALTED CYCLOPS AND ALL KLANSMEN.

GREETING:

Ever holding the best interest of the Invisible Empire, Knights of the Ku Klux Klan, in mind and heart, and having had committed to me the sacred trust of its government; I therefore, by virtue of the authority vested in me, do DECREE and OFFICIALLY PROCLAIM as follows,—

The Kloran is "THE book" of the Invisible Empire, and is therefore a sacred book with our citizens and its contents MUST be rigidly safeguarded and its teachings honestly respected.

The book or any part of it MUST not be kept or carried where any person of the "alien" world may chance to become acquainted with its sacred contents as such.

Its secrets MUST be held secure by you, and the prescribed "secret work" must not be used in any other than a legitimate manner. The signs MUST not be used only when necessary.

No innovation will be tolerated, and no frivolity or "horse-play" must be allowed during any ceremony.

All klansmen are required to study and imbibe its wholesome teachings and morally profit thereby. All klansmen are required to undergo an examination on the Kloran by the Exalted Cyclops of his respective klan, or another officer designated by him, before he can be an eligible applicant for knighthood.

I hereby enjoin upon all Exalted Cyclops and their Terrors to study CAREFULLY the kloranic INSTRUCTIONS given herein in light-face type; to commit to memory especially their respective parts, and to demonstrate same in ceremony in a graceful, forceful and dignified manner.

This decree is as binding as if its verbiage was incorporated in the Oath of Allegiance.

IN WARNING: A penalty sufficient will be speedily enforced for disregarding this decree in the profanation of the Kloran.

Done in the Aulic of His Majesty, the Imperial Wizard, Emperor of the Invisible Empire, Knights of the Ku Klux Klan, in the Imperial Palace, in the Imperial City of Atlanta, Commonwealth of Georgia, United States of America, this the 26th day of June, Anno Domini Nineteen Hundred and Sixteen, Anno Klan L.

Signed by His Majesty—

WILLIAM JOSEPH SIMMONS,
Imperial Wizard,

DIAGRAM OF KLAVERN

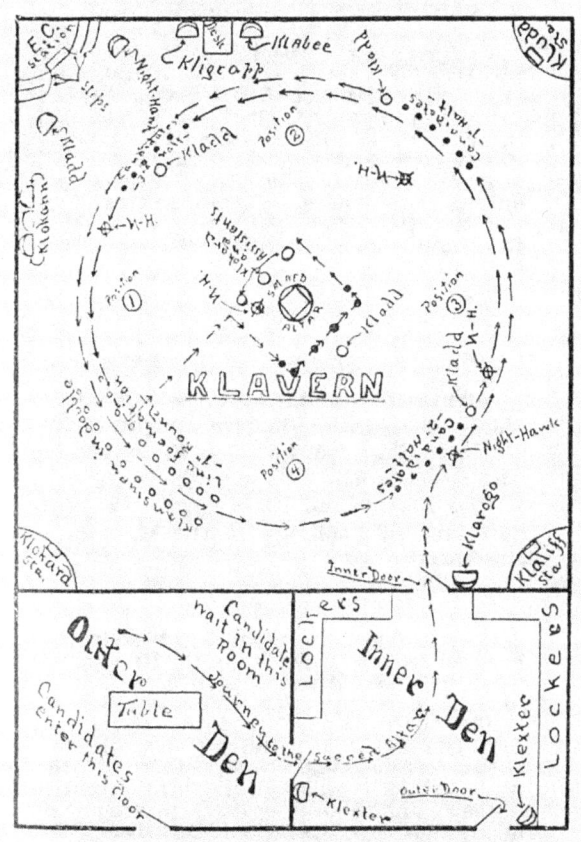

The official form of the Klavern is a perfect
quadrate, with the official stations in the
corners, as indicated above.

OPENING CEREMONY

KNIGHTS OF THE KU KLUX KLAN

Just prior to the opening of the klonklave, the Klaliff will procure the mounted flag and stand it at and in front of his station; the Klokard will procure the altar flag and the unsheathed sword and place same on his station with flag folded compactly; the Kludd will procure the vessel containing the dedication fluid and the bible and put same on his station, and the Night-Hawk will procure the Fiery Cross and stand it at and in front of the station of the E. C.

The time having arrived for the opening of the klonklave, the E. C. (in his absence his substitute) will ascend his station, and standing will give one rap with his gavel and say:

"All present who have not attained citizenship in the Invisible Empire, Knights of the Ku Klux Klan, will retire to the outer den under the escort of the Night-Hawk.

"The Klexter and Klarogo will take their posts and faithfully guard the entrance to this klavern."

*　　*　　*　　*　　*　　*　　*　　*

After all the applicants for citizenship shall have retired, the Klexter and the Klarogo will close their respective doors, the Klarogo making his secure. After this is done no one will be allowed to pass the Klarogo into the klavern until the klonklave is duly opened. All substitute officers shall be appointed at this point. The E. C. will then give three raps with his gavel and take his seat. (The officers do not assume their stations at this time.) The E. C. will then command—

E. C. "The Kladd of the Klan."

The Kladd will advance to a point about five

6

feet in front of the station of the E. C., salute and say:

Kladd. "The Kladd, your Excellency!"

E. C. "You will ascertain with care if all present are klansmen worthy to sit in the klavern during the deliberations of this klonklave."

Kladd. "I have your orders, Sir."

The Kladd will then collect from each Klansman present the countersign and password. As he approaches a Klansman, that Klansman will whisper the words into the ear of the Kladd and resume his seat immediately. If a Klansman should not have the word he will remain standing. The Kladd will proceed around the klavern to all present. After he has finished he will return to the E. C. and report as follows:

Kladd. "Your Excellency: I respectfully report that all present are klansmen worthy of the honor of sitting during the deliberations of this klonklave." (If any present have not the words, the Kladd will add to the above:) "Except those who stand before you; they presume to be klansmen, but they have not the words."

The E. C. will ascertain of the Kligrapp if the ones standing are worthy; if so, he will instruct them to advance to his station and procure the same. If they are not worthy all ceremony must cease until they become worthy or are ejected from the klavern. If there be visiting klansmen present they must be invited to the E. C. station at this time, met by him, then faced toward the sacred altar and introduced to the klan. All klansmen will arise and give the visiting klansmen Tsog. The visiting klansmen will respond with Tsog. This done the E. C. will give two raps with his gavel and say:

"My Terrors, you will take your respective stations as your names are called."

The E. O., sitting in his station, will call the roll of officers. When an officer's name is called, he will arise and answer: "**Here**," and proceed to his station, stand erect and face the sacred altar. (If an officer is absent his substitute will arise and call his own name, and say: "**Substitute**," and proceed to his station.) When the names of the Klexter and Night-Hawk are called the Klarogo will answer for them if they are present, but if either of them or both of them should be absent, the Klarogo will give the manes of their substitutes and so state.

No one will be allowed to sit on the station with an officer unless by consent of the E. O.

The E. O. will then arise; when he arises the Terrors will face him and salute; he will return the salute and charge them as follows:

"**My Terrors**: Your fellow klansmen hold you in high esteem. You have been chosen to fill an important place in the affairs of this klonklave and to set an example to all klansmen of perfect observance of our oath and dutiful devotion to our great fraternity. Therefore, I charge you to discharge every duty incumbent upon you with dispatch, efficiency and dignity. Preserve peace and observe due decorum in our deliberations at this time, and persevere with honor in promoting and guarding well every interest of the Invisible Empire, Knights of the Ku Klux Klan."

The E. O. will then give three raps and command:

E. O. "**My Terrors and Klansmen, make ready!**"

All will arise and put on their robes but leave their helmets off, and remain standing. (Robing may be omitted if there be no candidates

10

in waiting, in the discretion of the E. C.). He
will then say:

E. C. **"Prepare the sacred altar."**

The altar furnishings having been previously placed, the Klokard will advance to the
sacred altar from his station with altar flag
and sword; standing on side of sacred altar
next to Klaliff's station, he will spread the flag
across altar with stars to his left and on opposite edge of flag from him, and then place
directly across center of altar the sword, with
hilt toward the E. C. and takes position No. 1
(see diagram, p. 7) facing the sacred altar.

As he leaves the sacred altar, the Kludd will
advance to the sacred altar with Bible and vessel of dedication fluid; standing at point of
sword, he will place the Bible, opened at the
12th chapter of Romans, on and near the corner of sacred altar to his left and next to him,
and the vessel of fluid on and near the corner
of sacred altar to his right and opposite side
from him, and takes position No. 2 (see diagram, p. 7) and faces the sacred altar.

As he leaves the sacred altar, the Klaliff
will advance to the sacred altar with the
mounted flag and will stand flag directly out
from corner of sacred altar at his left and
about one foot from corner of sacred altar,
and take position No. 3 (see diagram, p. 7)
facing the sacred altar.

As he leaves the sacred altar, the Night-
Hawk (in his absence, the Kladd) will advance
to the sacred altar with the Fiery Cross and
place it at and against center of sacred altar
on side toward the E. C.'s station, light it,
and take position No. 4 (see diagram, p. 7)
facing the sacred altar.

The Klokard, from his position, carefully
surveys the sacred altar to make sure it is
properly prepared, corrects any imperfections
in its preparation, if any; from his position he
faces the E. C. (the other three Terrors will

11

do likewise) and addresses the E. C. as follows:

Klokard. "Your Excellency, the sacred altar of the klan is prepared, the fiery cross illumines the klavern."

E. C. "Faithful Klokard, why the fiery cross?"

Klokard. "Sir, it is the emblem of that sincere, unselfish devotedness of all klansmen to the sacred purpose and principles we have espoused."

E. C. "My Terrors and Klansmen, what means the fiery cross?"

All. "We serve and sacrifice for the right."

E. C. "Klansmen all: You will gather for our opening devotions."

When he says this he will arise and advance to and occupy position No. 2, occupied by the Kludd; as he approaches the Kludd, that Terror will advance to the sacred altar and take position near the point of sword. All klansmen will form on the quadrate, forming straight lines between these four positions; these four positions occupied by Terrors form the corners of the quadrate. The Terrors, in taking these positions, should step out far enough to accommodate the members between them, about an equal number on each side of quadrate. The distance between klansmen in this quadrate must be about three feet. If there be more than enough to form one line, the others will form back of the first line, and so on until all are in position. Great care must be exercised to form the quadrate correctly and symmetrically with the scared altar in as near the exact center as possible. When the formation is complete all will join in singing the following opening klode:

(The stanzas are sung to the tune of "From Greenland's Icy Mountains," and the chorus, "Home Sweet Home.")

I.

"We meet with cordial greetings
  In this our sacred cave
To pledge anew our compact
  With hearts sincere and brave;
A band of faithful Klansmen,
  Knights of the K. K. K.
We all will stand together
  Forever and for aye."

CHORUS.

"Home, home, country and home,
  Klansmen we'll live and die
For our country and home."

II.

"Here honor, love and justice
  Must actuate us all;
Before our sturdy phalanx
  All hate and strife shall fall.
In unison we'll labor
  Wherever we may roam
To shield a klansman's welfare,
  His country, name and home."

After singing, the Kludd at the sacred altar leads in the following prayer. (All must stand steady with heads reverently bowed.)

Our Father and our God. We, as klansmen, acknowledge our dependence upon Thee and Thy loving kindness toward us; may our gratitude be full and constant and inspire us to walk in Thy ways.

Give us to know that each Klansman by the

13

process of thought and conduct determines his own destiny, good or bad: May he forsake the bad and choose and strive for the good, remembering always that the living Christ is a Klansman's criterion of character.

Keep us in the blissful bonds of fraternal union, of clanish fidelity one toward another and of a devoted loyalty to this, our great Institution. Give us to know that the crowning glory of a klansman is to serve. Harmonize our souls with the sacred principles and purposes of our noble Order that we may keep our sacred oath inviolate, as Thou art our witness.

Bless those absent from our gathering at this time; Thy peace be in their hearts and homes.

God save our nation! And help us to be a nation worthy of existence on the earth. Keep ablaze in each Klansman's heart the sacred fire of a devoted patriotism to our country and its government.

We invoke Thy blessing upon our Emperor, the Imperial Wizard, and his official family, in the administrations of the affairs pertaining to the government of the Invisible Empire. Grant him wisdom and grace, and may each Klansman's heart and sould be inclined toward him in loving loyalty and unwavering devotion.

Oh, God! For Thy glory and our good we humbly ask these things in the name of Him who taught us to serve and sacrifice for the right. Amen. (All say "Amen.")

After the prayer, all facing the sacred altar, will give together **Tsog** and holding same will say, "**For my country, the Klan, my fellow Klansmen and my home.**" Then all give the

N. H. to the flag. The E. C. then immediately returns to his station; as he vacates position No. 2, the Kludd will advance from the sacred altar and occupy position No. 2; as the E. C. steps into his station, faces the assembly, and gives one rap with gavel, at this each klansman will face him and give **Tsotf-c**, then **Tsoc-l**, then raise **Tsos**, and then **Tsok-c**; as he responds with **Tsok-c** they will recover. He holds **Tsok-c** and says:

*   *   *   *   *   *   *   *

"**My** Terrors and Klansmen: In the sacred cause we have entered, be thou faithful unto death; be patriotic toward our country; be clanish toward Klansmen; be devoted to our great fraternity."

He then recovers **Tsok-c**, and says: **My** Terrors and Klansmen: What is the sworn duty of a Klansman in klonklave assembled?"

All answer in unison—"To maintain peace and harmony in all the deliberations of the Klan in klonklave assembled, and take heed to instructions given."

The E. C. will then give two raps with his gavel. After all are seated he will say:

E. C. "I now officially proclaim that this klonklave of _____Klan No. _____Realm of_____ of the Invisible Empire, Knights of the Ku Klux Klan, duly opened for the dispatch of business."

E. C. "Faithful Klarogo: You may now admit all qualified Klansmen, but guard well the portal to this klavern. The Night-Hawk (in his absence, the Kladd) **will extinguish the Fiery Cross.**"

He gives one rap with his gavel, takes his seat and proceeds with the regular order of business.

CLOSING CEREMONY

KNIGHTS OF THE KU KLUX KLAN

The order of business having been finished, the E. C. will arise, give one rap with his gavel and say:

"My Terrors and Klansmen: The sacred purpose of the gathering of the klan at this time has been fulfilled; the deliberations of this klonklave have ended."

E. C. "Faithful Klaliff: What is the four-fold duty of a Klansman?"

The Klaliff will arise and say:

Klaliff. "To worship God; be patriotic toward our country; be devoted and loyal to our Klan and Emperor, and to practice clanishness toward his fellow klansmen." (And remains standing.)

E. C. "Faithful Kludd: How speaketh the oracles of our God?"

The Kludd will arise and say:

Kludd. "Thou shalt worship the Lord thy God. Render unto the state the things which are the state's. Love the brotherhood: honor the king. Bear ye one another's burdens, and so fulfill the law of Christ." (And remains standing.)

E. C. "Faithful Klokard: What does a Klansman value more than life?"

The Klokard will arise and say:

Klokard. "Honor to a Klansman is more than life." (And remains standing.)

16

E. C. "Faithful Klaliff: How is a Klansman to preserve his honor?"

Klaliff. "By the discharge of duty in the faithful keeping of his oath." (And remains standing.)

E. C. "What say you, my Terrors?"

All the other officers will arise and say in unison:

Officers. "Your Excellency: The immaculate truth has been spoken." (And remain standing.)

E. C. "What say you, my fellow Klansmen?"

All members will arise and say in unison:

Members. "Amen!" (And remain standing.)

E. C. "My Terrors and Klansmen: You know well the duty of a Klansman; be thou not recreant to duty's demands as we go hence from this klavern to enter the stressful struggle of the alien world. Protect your honor by keeping inviolate your sacred oath."

The E. C. then gives one rap with his gavel, and gives the Sok-c, which is answered by all. All will recover the Sok-c together.

E. C. "The crowning glory of a Klansman s to serve, 'Non Silba Sed Anthar." (All will say: "Not for self but for others.") "Let us e faithful in serving our God, our country, our Emperor and our fellow klansmen."

* * * * * * *

The E. C. will then give one rap with his gavel and say:

E. C. "My Faithful Klansmen: As peace dwells among us you will assemble for our parting devotions."

All will assemble on the quadrate formed as in opening ceremony (the Klarogo and Klexter making secure their respective doors); the Kludd stands at the sacred altar. All will stand facing the sacred altar and come to the Sotf-c, and resting palms on back of each other, thus paralleling the **Ars**, and will join in singing the following closing klode:

(Tune Dennis—S. M.)

All Standing.

I.

"Blest be the Klansman's tie
Of real fraternal love,
That binds us in a fellowship
Akin to that above."

Each will then stand with left hand over the heart and the right resting on the left shoulder of the klansman to the right.

E. C. "Klansmen: United in the sacred bond of klanish fidelity we stand, but divided by selfishness and strife we fall; shall we stand, or shall we fall?"

All will answer:

"We will stand; for our blood is not pledged in vain."

Each klansman will then sing the following Kloxology:

18

(Tune—America)

"God of Eternity
   Guard, guide our great country,
   Our homes and store.
   Keep our great state to Thee,
   Its people right and free.
   In us Thy glory be,
   Forevermore."

After the singing all look toward the mounted flag and will **Gtnh** and then stand with bowed heads; the Kludd standing at the sacred altar will pronounce the following benediction:

The Benediction.

"May the blessings of our God wait upon thee and the sun of glory shine around thy head; may the gates of plenty, honor, and happiness be always open to thee and thine, so far as they will not rob thee of eternal joys.

"May no strife disturb thy days, nor sorrow distress thy nights, and when death shall summons thy departure may the Saviour's blood have washed thee from all impurities, perfected thy initiation, and thus prepared, enter thou into the Empire Invisible and repose thy soul in perpetual peace."

"Amen!" (All say, "Amen.")

The benediction having been pronounced the E. C. will immediately return to his station, give one rap with his gavel and say:

E. C. "I now officially proclaim that this klonklave of_____Klan No.____ Realm of_____of the Invisible Empire, Knights of the Ku Klux Klan, duly

19

closed. The Klan will gather again in (regular or special) klonklave_____night."

He will then say:

E. C. "Klansmen, One and All." Saying this he Ltsos, which all will do likwise. All will then give and hold Tsog, and the E. C. will say:

E. C. "To you, faithful Klansmen, good night!" All will say: "Your Excellency, good night!" He and they will recover Tsog together. The E. C. gives one rap and announces:

"The Kladd and the Night-Hawk will gather and make secure the properties of the klan."

"The klan is dismissed. Faithful Klarogo: you will open the portal that all klansmen may pass to the outer world."

On going out each klansman MUST see to it that the robe and helmet worn by him is carefully and properly placed in locker or other place for safe keeping, if he does not carry same home with him by permission of the E. C.

NATURALIZATION CEREMONY

KNIGHTS OF THE KU KLUX KLAN

When the ceremony of naturalization shall have been reached in the regular order of business, the Klarogo will signal by **Allw** to the Klexter, who will repeat the signal to the Night-Hawk in the outer den with candidates. Prior to the signal the Night-Hawk will have presented a blank Petition of Citizenship to each candidate, requesting him to read and sign same. (Said petition to be witnessed by the Night-Hawk.) He will collect from each candidate the klectokon, if same has not been previously paid. On hearing the signal of the Klexter he will excuse himself from the candidates and will approach the outer door of the inner den and give thereon seven raps (having in his possession the petition of the candidates and the klectokons by him collected).

Klexter. "Who dares to approach so near the entrance of this klavern?"

N.-H. "The Night-Hawk of the klan."

Klexter. "Advance with the countersign."

(The N.-H. will then give the countersign in a low whisper through the wicket.)

Klexter. (Will open the outer door and say) "Pass."

The N.-H. passes the outer door into the inner den of the klavern and at once enrobes completely and then approaches and signals on the inner door * * * * X. The Klarogo will open the wicket. When the wicket is opened the N.-H. will **Gallw**.

Klarogo. "Who seeks entrance to the klavern?"

N.-H. "The Night-Hawk of the klan with

important information and documents from the alien world for His Excellency.''

The Klarogo secures the wicket, salutes and reports to the E. C.

Klarogo. "Your Excellency: The Night-Hawk of the klan is respectfully waiting to enter the klavern with important information and documents from the alien world.''

E. C. "You will permit him to enter.''

Klarogo. (Through the wicket **Gallw**, which is answered by the N.-H. with **Allw**, and gives the password through the wicket.) Then the Klarogo opens the door and says: "**You have His Excellency's permission to enter.**" The N. H. enters, steps across the threshold of the klavern, stands erect and **Gtsog**; all will answer by the same from their seats. The N.-H. will then proceed to the altar. Arriving at the altar, he **Gtnh**, then **Gtsof-c**, then removes his helmet and **Gtsok-c**, and stands erect and steady.

* * * * * * * *

E. C. "Faithful Night-Hawk, you may now speak and impart to us the important information in your possession.''

N.-H. (Bows and speaks.) "Your Excellency: Sir, pursuant to my duty in seeking laudable adventure in the alien world, I found these men (Here he gives their names). They having read the Imperial Proclamation of our Emperor, and prompted by unselfish motives, desire a nobler life. In consequence they have made the honorable decision to forsake the world of selfishness and fraternal alienation and emigrate to the delectable bounds of the Invisible Empire and become loyal citizens of the same.''

E. C. "Faithful Night-Hawk: This is indeed important information, and most pleasant to hear. Important, in that it evidences human progress; most pleasant, in that it reveals through you a klansman's sincere appreciation of his sacred mission among men and his fidelity to duty in the betterment of mankind. Their respective petitions will be received and justly considered."

N.-H. (Bows and says): "Sir, I have in my possession the required petitions for citizenship of the men named, together with their klectokon."

E. C. "Then you will approach and deliver same to the Kligrapp who will publish them to all klansmen in klonklave assembled."

The N.-H. will deliver the petitions and klectokons to the Kligrapp and resume his position at the altar. The Kligrapp will then arise and publish the names of the petitioners and hand the petitions to the E. C. and resume his seat. The E. C. will say:

E. C. "Klansmen, you have heard the publication of the petition for citizenship in the Invisible Empire of (here he gives the names). Does any klansman, on his oath of allegiance, know of any just reason why these aliens, or any of them, should be denied citizenship in the Invisible Empire?"

* * * * * * * *

If there be no objections, the E. C. will address the Night-Hawk:

E. C. "Faithful Night-Hawk, you will inform these alien petitioners from me:
"That it is the constant disposition of a

23

klansman to assist those who aspire to things noble in thought and conduct, and to extend a helping hand to the worthy. That their desires are sincerely respected, their manly petitions are being seriously considered in the light of justice and honor. With true faith a man may expect a just answer to his prayers and his virtuous hopes will ultimately ripen into a sublime fruition."

The Night-Hawk bows and says: "I have your orders, Sir," and retires to the outer door of the inner den of the klavern and through the wicket of the outer door informs the candidates as follows:

N.-H. "Worthy Aliens: His Excellency, the Exalted Cyclops, being the direct representative of His Majesty, our Emperor, and chief guardian of the portal of the Invisible Empire, has officially instructed me to inform you that it is the constant disposition of a klansman to assist those who aspire to things noble in thought and conduct and to extend a helping hand to the worthy. Therefore your desires are sincerely respected and your manly petitions are being seriously considered in the light of justice and honor. With true faith you may expect a just answer to your prayers, and your virtuous hopes will ultimately ripen into a sublime fruition. This is the decision of His Excellency, the Exalted Cyclops, with all his klan concurring."

The Night-Hawk returns to his station in the klavern without form.

E. C. "Faithful Klokard: You will examine under witness the alien petitioners, as to their qualifications."

24

The Klokard, with his assistants, the Klaliff and the Kludd, retires to the outer den and will propound to the candidates in waiting the following required "Qualifying Interrogatories," and then immediately administer Sections I and II of the "Oath of Allegiance;" requiring each candidate to place his left hand over his heart and raise his right hand to heaven.

Qualifying Interrogatories.

The Klokard will first ask each candidate his name and then speak to the candidates in the outer den as follows:

"Sirs: The Knights of the Ku Klux Klan, as a great and essentially a patriotic, fraternal, benevolent Order, does not discriminate against a man on account of his religious or political creed, when same does not conflict with or antagonize the sacred rights and privileges guaranteed by our civil government, and Christian ideals and institutions.

Therefore, to avoid any misunderstanding and as evidence that we do not seek to impose unjustly the requirements of this Order upon anyone who cannot, on account of his religious or political scruples, voluntarily meet our requirements and faithfully practice our principles, and as proof that we respect all honest men in their sacred convictions, whether same are agreeable with our requirements or not, we require as an absolute necessity on the part of each of you an affirmative answer to each of the following questions:

Each of the following questions must be answered by (each of) you with an emphatic "Yes."

1st. Is the motive prompting your ambition to be a klansman serious and unselfish?......

25

2nd. Are you a native-born white, Gentile American citizen? _____

3rd. Are you absolutely opposed to and free of any allegiance of any nature to any cause, government, people, sect or ruler that is foreign to the United States of America? _____

4th. Do you believe in the tenets of the Christian religion? _____

5th. Do you esteem the United States of America and its institutions above any other government, civil, political or ecclesiastical, in the whole world? _____

6th. Will you, without mental reservation, take a solemn oath to defend, preserve and enforce same? _____

7th. Do you believe in clanishness and will you faithfully practice same towards klansmen? _____

8th. Do you believe in and will you faithfully strive for the eternal maintenance of white supremacy? _____

9th. Will you faithfully obey our constitution and laws, and conform willingly to all our usages, requirements and regulations? _____

10th. Can you be always depended on? _____

He then administers Sections I and II of the oath.

*　　*　　*　　*　　*　　*　　*　　*

This done, he, with his assistants, will return to the sacred altar, he will salute and report as follows: "Your Excellency: (Here

26

state the number of petitioners) ...... men in waiting have each duly qualified to enter our klavern to journey through the mystic cave in quest of citizenship in the Invisible Empire." .

E. C. "Faithfull Klokard, you and your assistants will resume your stations."

E. C. "The Kladd of the klan!" The Kladd will arise and advance to a position immediately in front of the E. C., and about five feet from his station, and salute and say:

Kladd. "The Kladd, Your Excellency!"

E. C. "You will retire under special orders to the outer premises of the klavern, assume charge of the worthy aliens in waiting, and afford them a safe journey from the world of selfishness and fraternal alienation to the sacred altar of the empire of chivalry, industry, honor and love."

Kladd. Salutes the E. C. and says: "I have your orders, Sir!" He retires to the room where the candidates are. Lines them up in single file, the left hand of the rear man on the left shoulder of the man in front. He then takes his place in front of them and says: "Follow me and be (a man) men!" He proceeds to the outer door of the inner den and gives thereon * O.

Klexter. (Opens the wicket and says): "Who and what is your business?"

Kladd. "I am the Kladd of Klan No........ Realm of......., acting under special orders of His Excellency, our Exalted Cyclops; I am in charge of a party!"

Klexter. "What be the nature of your party?"

Kladd. "Worthy aliens from the world of selfishness and fraternal alienation prompted by unselfish motive, desire the honor of citizenship in the Invisible Empire and the fellowship of klansmen."

Klexter. "Has your party been selected with care?"

Kladd. "These men (or this man) are (or is) known and vouched for by klansmen in klonklave assembled."

Klexter. "Have they (or has he) the marks?"

Kladd. "The distinguishing marks of a klansman are not found in the fibre of his garments or his social or financial standing, but are spiritual; namely, a chivalric head, a compassionate heart, a prudent tongue and a courageous will. All devoted to our country, our klan, our homes and each other; these are the distinguishing marks of a klansman, oh, Faithful Klexter! And these men claim the marks."

Klexter. "What if one of your party should prove himself a traitor?"

Kladd. "He would be immediately banished in disgrace from the Invisible Empire without fear or favor, conscience would tenaciously torment him, remorse would repeatedly revile him, and direful things would befall him."

Klexter. "Do they (or does he) know all this?"

Kladd. "All this he (or they) now know. He (or they) has (or have) heard, and they must heed."

Klexter. "Faithful Kladd: You speak the truth."

Kladd. "Faithful Klexter: A Klansman speaketh the truth in and from his heart. A lying scoundrel may wrap his disgraceful frame within the sacred folds of a klansman's robe and deceive the very elect, but only a klansman possesses a klansman's heart and a klansman's soul."

Klexter. "Advance with the countersign."

The Kladd advances and whispers the countersign through the wicket to the Klexter.

Klexter. (Opens the door and says): "With heart and soul, I, the Klexter of the Klan, welcome you and open the way for you to attain the most noble achievement in your earthly career. Be faithful and true unto death and all will be well and your reward will be sure. Noble Kladd, pass with your party!"

The Kladd, with his party will pass the outer door and stop. He then will give **Allw.** The Klarogo, upon hearing the **Llw**, will announce:

Klarogo. "**Your Excellency and klansmen assembled. I hear from the watch the signal of the Kladd of the klan with a party!**"

* * * * * * * *

E. C. "**My Terrors and Klansmen, one and all; make ready!**"

Each klansman present will put on his helmet, both aprons dropped down, robes completely buttoned and girdles tied and capes adjusted; all lights must be turned down so as to make the klavern almost dark. All must remain as still and as quiet as possible; there must be no moving, talking or noise only as the ceremony requires. Striking matches and smoking during the ceremony is absolutely

29

prohibited. If an officer has to read he must use an electric flash-light, and throw the light only on the page he is reading. When all are ready the Klarogo will answer the signal of the Kladd with **Allw** and begin to **Otds**.

Kladd. (On **Stdos** the Kladd will say to his party): "Sirs: **The portal of the Invisible Empire is being opened for you. Your righteous prayer has been answered and you have found favor in the sight of the Exalted Cyclops and his klansmen assembled. Follow me and be prudent!**"

As the Kladd approaches with his party the threshold of the inner door, the Klarogo will stop them by facing them with **Tsotf-c,** He will then recover **Tsotf-c,** face inward and stand erect and steady. (The Klokard, or person selected, just previous to this has stationed himself near the door where he can be heard by the candidates but not seen by them.) Klokard—

"God give us men! The Invisible Empire demands strong
Minds, great hearts, true faith and ready hands.
Men whom the lust of office does not kill;
Men whom the spoils of office cannot buy;
Men who possess opinions and a will;
Men who have HONOR; men who will NOT Lie;
Men who can stand before a demagogue
And damn his treacherous flatteries without winking!
Tall men, sun-crowned, who live above the fog
In public duty and in private thinking;
For while the rabble, with their thumb-worn creeds,

Their LARG E professions and their LITTLE deeds,

30

Mingle in selfish strife, Lo! freedom weeps
Wrong rules the land, and waiting justice
  sleeps.
God give us men!
Men who serve not for selfish booty.
But real men, courageous, who flinch not at
  duty;
Men of dependable character; men of sterling
  worth;
Then wrongs will be redressed, and right will
  rule the earth;
God give us men!"

After a pause, the Klarogo faces the candidates and says:

Klarogo. "Sirs: Will you (or each of you) by your daily life as klansmen earnestly endeavor to be an answer to this prayer? _ _ _ _ _

He then faces the E. C. and says:

Klarogo. "Your Excellency and fellow klansmen: JUST SUCH MEN are (or just such a man is) standing without the portal of the Invisible Empire, desiring the lofty honor of citizenship therein, and ready and willing to unflinchingly face every duty on him (or them) imposed. "

*   *   *   *   *   *   *   *

E. C. "Faithful Klarogo and klansmen: Let them enter the klavern in quest of citizenship, but keep you a klansman's eye of scrutiny upon them, and if they, or one of them, should flinch at duty or show himself a cowardly weakling or a treacherous scalawag, at this time or in the future, it will be your sworn duty to eject him or them from the portal of the Invisible Empire without fear or favor and do so without delay; be thou not recreant to duty's demands!"

While the above prayer is being said the Night-Hawk takes the Fiery Cross from the altar, lights it and takes a position immediately in front of and about four feet from the Klaliff's station, facing the Klarogo, holding the Fiery Cross above his head.

Klarogo. (Steps aside and says to the Kladd): "Pass."

When the Kladd crosses the threshold of the klavern he will stop and give **Tsog**. All klansmen, except the station officers, will arise, face the Kladd and give **Tsog**, then face the altar and remain standing with **Tsoc-l**. The Kladd will then proceed with his party toward the N.-H. As the Kladd approaches the N.-H. with his party and gets in about six feet of him the Night-Hawk will about face and march in front of the Kladd about six feet from him on the journey, until he is halted by the signal **Allw** from the E. C. When he hears the signal he will stop his party, answer the signal with **Allw**, then face his party toward the sacred altar. When this is done the Night-Hawk with the Fiery Cross takes a position in front of and about six feet from the party, facing the party with the Cross uplifted. He remains in this position until he hears the second signal of **Allw** from the E. C., when he will resume his position at the head of the party in front of the Kladd and move on. When the Kladd hears the second signal he will face his party as they were, answer the signal with **Allw**, and follow the N.-H.

When the first signal of **Allw** of the E. C. is given, all klansmen, except the station ofcers, Klarogo and Klexter, will form from their seats, march around the hall in single file, the Klokard leading to his right, pass in front along the line of the party, between the party and the N.-H., each klansman will look the party squarely in the eyes, but continue moving; after passing the party the Klokard will form the klansmen in a double line with open

32

ranks about six feet apart and facing each other, holding **Tsoc-l**, and standing steady, on the opposite side of the klavern; the E. C. then gives the second signal of **Allw.** The Night-Hawk will lead the Kladd and his party on their journey by way of the E. C. station and through the formation of klansmen. All this must be done quietly, with dignity and with a steady pace.

After the Kladd and his party shall have passed the formation of klansmen, all klansmen will, without signal, return to their seats, but remain standing until the Kladd presents his party to the E. C., when they quietly sit down.

As the Kladd approaches the station of the Klaliff after he has passed the formation of klansmen, the Klaliff will arise and **Gtsog** and halt him with **Allw.** On hearing the **Llw**, the Kladd stops and answers with same. The N.-H. also stops.

Klaliff. "Who are you that walk in the klavern at this hour?"

Kladd. "The Kladd of the klan with a party, whom the eye of the unknown has seen and doth constantly observe."

Klaliff. "What be the nature of your party?"

Kladd. "Faithful Klaliff: THESE ARE MEN, (or this is a man) as the Invisible Empire and a time like this demands; men (a man) of strong minds, great hearts, true faith and ready hands. Worthy aliens known and vouched for by klansmen in klonklave assembled, and by order of His Excellency, I, the Kladd of the klan, am their (or his) guide to the sacred altar."

Klaliff. "Pass on "

(The journey from the entrance of the klavern to the E. C. station must be made in a circle around the klavern.)

33

The N.-H. will move on, followed by the Kladd with his party, and will then continue his journey until he arrives at the station of the E. C., when he shall stop and line his company up in a straight line immediately in front of the station. The Night-Hawk stops but does not change position. The Kladd steps to the rear of his party and will address the E. C. as follows:

*   *   *   *   *   *   *   *

Kladd. "Your Excellency Sir, pursuant to your orders, I present to you these (or this) alien aspirants, men (or a man) of dependable character and courage, who aspire to the noble life and the high honor of citizenship in the Invisible Empire."

The Exalted Cyclops will arise and address the candidates as follows:

"Sirs: Is the motive prompting youre presence here serious and unselfish?......

"It is indeed refreshing to meet face to face with men (or a man) like you, who, actuated by manly motives, aspire to all things noble for yourselves and humanity.

"The lustre of the holy light of chivalry has lost its former glory and is sadly dimmed by the choking dust of selfish, sordid gain. Pass on!"   .

The E. C. will resume his seat, and the Kladd will face his party toward the Night-Hawk and advance behind the Night-Hawk until he hears the signal of Allw from the Klokard. On hearing the signal from the Klokard the Night-Hawk stops and stands steady; the Kladd will also stop his party immediately in front of the Klokard's station and face them to the Klokard's station and answer the signal by the same. On receiving the answer, the

34

Klokard will arise and address the party as follows:

"Real fraternity, by shameful neglect, has been starved until so weak her voice is lost in the courts of her own castle, and she passes unnoticed by her sworn subjects as she moves along the crowded streets and through the din of the market place. Man's valuation of man is by the standard of wealth and not worth; selfishness is the festive queen among human kind, and multitudes forget honor, justice, love and God and every religious conviction to do homage to her, and yet with the cruel heart of Jezebel she slaughters the souls of thousands of her devotees daily. Pass on!"

The Klokard will resume his seat, and the Kladd will face his party as before and advance behind the Night-Hawk until he hears the signal of **Allw** from the Klaliff. On hearing the signal of the Klaliff the Night-Hawk stops and stands steady; the Kladd will also stop his party immediately in front of the Klaliff's station, facing them to the Klaliff, and answer the signal by the same. On receiving the answer, the Klaliff will arise and address the party as follows:

"The unsatiated thirst for gain is dethroning reason and judgment in the citadel of the human soul, and men maddened thereby, forget their patriotic, domestic and social obligations and duties, and fiendishly fight for a place in the favor of the goddess of glittering gold; they starve their own souls, and make sport of spiritual development. Pass on "

The Klaliff will resume his seat, and the Kladd will face his party as before and advance behind the Night-Hawk until he hears

35

the signal of **Allw** from the Kludd. On hearing the signal of the Kludd, the Night-Hawk stops and stands steady; the Kladd will also stop his party immediately in front of the Kludd's station, facing them to the Kludd, and then answers the signal by the same. On receiving the answer, the Kludd will arise and address the party as follows:

"Men speak of love and live in hate!,
Men talk of faith and trust to fate!,
Oh, might men do the things they teach
Oh, might men live the life they preach
Then the throne of avarice would fall and
the clangor
Of grim Selfishness o'er the earth would
cease;
Love would tread out the baleful fire of
anger,
And in its ashes plant the lily of peace.
"Pass on"

The Kludd will resume his seat, and the Kladd will face his party as before and advance behind the Night-Hawk until he hears the signal of **Allw** from the E. C. On hearing the signal of the E. C. the Night-Hawk stops and goes to and takes position at the sacred altar; the Kladd will also stop his party immediately in front of the E. C.'s station, facing them to the E. C., and then answer the signal with the same. On receiving the answer, the E. C. will arise and address the party as follows:

"Sirs: We congratulate you on your manly decision to forsake the world of selfishness and fraternal alienation and emigrate to the delectable bounds of the Invisible Empire and become loyal citizens of the same. The prime purpose of this great Order is to develop character, practice clanishness, to protect the home and the chastity of womanhood, and to exemplify a pure patriotism towards our glorious country.

36

You, as citizens of the Invisible Empire, must be actively patriotic toward our country and constantly clanish toward klansmen socially, physically, morally and vocationally; will you assume this obligation of citizenship? ......

You must unflinchingly conform to our requirements, regulations and usages in every detail, and prove yourselves worthy to have and to hold the honors we bestow; do you freely and faithfully assume to do this? ......

Sirs: If you have any doubt as to your ability to qualify, either in body or character, as citizens of the Invisible Empire, you now have an opportunity to retire from this place with the good will of the klan to attend you; for I warn you now, if you falter or fail at this time or in the future as a klansman, in klonklave or in life, you will be banished from citizenship in the Invisible Empire without fear or favor.

This is a serious undertaking; we are not here to make sport of you, nor indulge in the silly frivolity of circus clowns. Be you well assured that "he that putteth his hand to the plow and looketh back is not fit for the kingdom of heaven," or worthy of the high honor of citizenship in the Invisible Empire, or the fervent fellowship of klansmen. Don't deceive yourselves; you cannot deceive us, and we will not be mocked. Do you wish to retire? ......

E. C. "Faithful Kladd, you will direct the way for these worthy aliens to the sacred altar of the empire of chivalry, honor, industry and love, in order that they may make further progress toward attaining citizenship in the Invisible Empire, Knights of the Ku Klux Klan."

The Kladd will conduct his party to the sacred altar by way of the Klokard's station. When he has arrived within about six feet of the Klokard's station he will turn square to his left and continue in a straight direction until he reaches a point about six feet of the sacred altar toward the station of the E. C.; he will then turn square to his right and continue until he has passed the sacred altar about four feet; he will then turn square to his left and continue until he passes the sacred alter about six feet when he will turn square to his left and bring his party into the formation of a three-quarter hollow square, and will face them towards the sacred altar.

If he has five candidates or a fewer number he will form them in a straight line facing the sacred altar on the side of the altar toward the Klaliff's station and about four feet from the altar, and then perfect the three-quarter hollow square formation with klansmen.

The N.-H. takes his place with the Fiery Cross held aloft just from the corner of the sacred altar to the right of the E. C. He stands within the quadrate. The Fiery Cross is held aloft during the administration of the oath and dedicatory ceremony.

The first paragraph above gives a general idea regarding the journey of the candidates to the sacred altar as to turning angles and as to distances, etc. In making this journey the number of candidates and the good judgment of the Kladd will determine the size of the hollow square formation and the best results in getting to and forming it.

The Kladd should study well his part in the floor work, for his is a very important and impressive part. He should exercise good military mannerisms in his work.

When the Kladd has perfected the three-quarter hollow square formation, he will advance to a point about midway between the altar and the station of the E. C., salute and in a strong, clear voice say:

Kladd. "Your Excellency: The aliens in ou midst from the world of selfishness and fraternal alienation, forsake the past and are now ready and willing to bind themselves by an unyielding tie to the Invisible Empire, Knights of the Ku Klux Klan."

Then the Kladd will about face and advance to his position opposite of the center and to the rear of the line of candidates toward the station of the Klaliff and await orders.

The Klokard, with his assistants, the Klaliff and the Kludd, will, with steady pace, form across the open side of the hollow square so as to complete the square, and will administer Sections III and IV of the Oath of Allegiance. The Klaliff administers Section III, and the Kludd administers Section IV. The Klokard stands between his assistants, the Klaliff to his right, the Kludd to his left. After the Oath shall have been administered, the Klokard will about face and advance to a point about midway between the altar and the E. C., facing the E. C.; he will salute and address the E. C. thus:

Klokard. "Your Excellency: The worthy aspirants at the sacred altar of the klan have each voluntarily assumed, without mental reservation the solemn and thrice binding Oath of Allegiance to the Invisible Empire, Knights of the Ku Klux Klan, and are awaiting to be dedicated to the holy service of our country, the klan, each other, our homes and humanity."

E. C. "Faithful Klokard: You and your assistants have performed your duty well; now you may rest; but stand by in readiness to perform other duties, if such arise."

The Klokard resumes his place in the quadrate formation between his assistants. The E. C. will then proceed to the sacred altar to perform the following ceremony of dedication:

DEDICATION.

The E. C. addresses the candidates as follows:

E. C. "Sirs: Have (each of) you assumed without mental reservation your Oath of Allegiance to the Invisible Empire? _____

Mortal man cannot assume a more binding oath; character and courage alone will enable you to keep it. Always remember that to keep this oath means to you honor, happiness and life; but to violate it means disgrace, dishonor and death. May honor, happiness and life be yours."

   *   *   *   *   *   *   *   *

(Then he holds up the vessel from the sacred altar, containing the dedication fluid, and addresses the candidates as follows):

"With this transparent, life-giving, powerful God-given fluid, more precious and far more significant than all the sacred oils of the ancients, I set you (or each of you) apart from the men of your daily association to the great and honorable task you have voluntarily allotted yourselves as citizens of the Invisible Empire, Knights of the Ku Klux Klan.

"As a klansman may your character be as transparent, your life purpose as powerful, your motive in all things as magnanimous and as pure, and your clanishness as real and as faithful as the manifold drops herein, and you a vital being as useful to humanity as is pure water to mankind.

"You will kneel upon your right knee."

Just here the following stanza must be sung in a low, soft, but distinct tone, preferably by a quartette:

40

(Tune—"Just As I Am Without One Plea.")

To Thee, oh, God I call to Thee—
True to my oath, oh, help me be!
I've pledged my love, my blood, my all;
Oh, give me grace that I not fall.

*   *   *   *   *   *   *   *

E. C. "Sirs: 'Neath the uplifted fiery cross which by its holy light looks down upon you to bless with its sacred traditions of the past,—

I dedicate you in body, in mind, in spir't and in life, to the holy service of our country, our klan, our homes, each other and humanity."

He advances to the candidates and pours a few drops of the dedication fluid on each candidate's back and says: **"In Body,"** pours a few drops on his head and says: **"In Mind,"** places a few drops on his own hand and tosses it upward and says: **"In Spirit,"** then moves his hand in a horizontal circular motion around the candidate's head and says: **"And in Life."** After this he says:

"Thus dedicated by us, now consecrate yourselves to the sacred cause you have entered."

(To all he will say): **"My Terrors and Klansmen: Let us pray."**

All except those officiating at the sacred altar must kneel, the E. C. will step back to the rear and left of the Kludd; the N.-H. remains in his position; the Kludd will advance and stand close to the sacred altar on the side toward the station of the E. C., and will use the following

DEDICATORY PRAYER

God of all, author of all good: Thou who didst create man and so proposed that man should fill a distinct place and perform a specific work in the economy of Thy good government, Thou has revealed Thyself and Thy

purpose to man, and by this revelation we
have learned our place and our work. Therefore, we have solemnly dedicated ourselves as
klansmen to that sublime work harmonic with
Thy will and purpose in our creation.

Now, oh, God! We, through Thy goodness,
have here dedicated with Thine own divinely
distilled fluid these manly men at the altar
kneeling, who have been moved by worthy
motives and impelled by noble impulses to
turn from selfishness and fraternal alienation and to espouse with body, mind, spirit
and life, the holy service of our country, our
klan, our home and each other,—we beseech
Thee to dedicate them with the fullness of
Thy spirit, keep him (or each of them) true to
his (or their) sacred, solemn oath to our noble
cause, to the glory of Thy great name. Amen!
(All say, "Amen!")

Immediately after the prayer all will arise.
The E. C. will step to the altar and instruct the
candidates to arise. The Kludd will step back
to his place.

*   *   *   *   *   *   *   *

(The E. C. will address the candidates as
follows):

"Sir (or Sirs): You are no longer strangers
or aliens among us, but are citizens with us;
and with confidence in your character that
you have not sworn falsely or deceitfully in the
assumption of your oath, I, on behalf of our
Emperor and all klansmen, welcome you to
citizenship in the empire of chivalry, honor,
industry and love."

After saying this the E. C. will raise the
front apron of his helmet (and all klansmen

42

will do the smae) and as a token of welcome he will greet each of the candidates with **Tcok,** and then returns to his position at the altar and says:

"By authority vested in me by our Emperor, I now declare and proclaim (each of) you a citizen of the Invisible Empire, Knights of the Ku Klux Klan, and invest you with the title of—'Klansman,' the most honorable title among men."

This done the E. C. returns to his station and the candidate is greeted under the Fiery Cross by all klansmen with **Tcok,** the Klaliff leading the line.

This done, the Night-Hawk will extinguish the Fiery Cross and replace it at the altar and take his seat. The Klarogo will have turned on the lights of the klavern; this done, the E. C. will say:

E. C. "The Kladd of the klan."

The Kladd will advance from his position at the rear of the candidates to a point about five feet in front of the E. C. and salute and say:

Kladd. "The Kladd, Your Excellency."

E. C. "You will escort the klansmen at the sacred altar to the station of the Klokard that they may receive instructions in the Way of the Klavern."

Kladd. (The Kladd will salute and say): "I have your orders, Sir!"

The Kladd conducts the candidates and forms them in a straight line in front of the Klokard where seats have been provided, and will instruct them to be seated. He will take a position at the center and to the rear of the candidates and remain standing while the instructions are being given.

THE WAY OF THE KLAVERN.

You will approach the outer door of the inner den and give thereon one rap and strike the O., the Klexter will answer with the same. He then will open the wicket and you will **Gaslw.** He will say, **"Who are you?"** You will give him your name as Klansman........ giving the name, number and realm of your klan. He will say: **"Advance and give the countersign."** You will advance and whisper the countersign through the wicket. If you haven't the countersign you will so inform the Klexter and produce your receipt, or otherwise satisfy him that you are no imposter. If you are qualified to enter he will open the door and say to you—"Pass."

You will pass into the inner den and say: **"Klexter, what of the night?"** If there be candidates to be initiated or already present he will say, **"Strangers are near; be prudent!"** On hearing this you will completely enrobe before entering the klavern. But if there be no candidates, and no initiatory work to be done, he will say, **"All are known."** Hearing this you will not robe but enter as you are.

*   *   *   *   *   *   *   *

You will then approach the inner door and give thereon * * * * you will then strike the F. C.; at this the Klarogo will open the wicket and say: **"Who is it and what is your business?"** You will answer: "I am Klansman ----------------------------; I seek entrance to the klavern to meet with my fellows." If necessary he will demand your receipt or ascertain of the Kligrapp if you are entitled to enter; if so, he will then open the wicket and say, **"Password."** If same is correct, he will open the door and say, **"Pass, Klansman."**

You will pass clear of the door, stop, stand erect and **Gtsog** and hold same until someone answers it; then pass on to the sacred altar, face the station of the E. C., then face the mounted flag and **Gtnh**; then face the E. C. and **Gtsof-c**; then raise **Tsos** if you are not enrobed; if you are robed you will remove your

44

helmet instead of raising **Tsos**; then **Gtsok-c**, which will be answered by the Exalted Cyclops with **Tsor**; you then will take your seat. If you are robed and the others have their helmets on disguised, you will not remove your helmet, but will take your seat without disclosing your identity. If the Exalted Cyclops is engaged you will give **Tsok-c** to the Klaliff.

To retire from the klavern while same is in session, you will advance to the sacred altar, face the Exalted Cyclops and lower **Tsos**, or put on your helmet; then **Gtsok-c**; if he answers you with **Tsog**, you may retire. If the Exalted Cyclops does not answer you, you must raise **Tsos** and return to your seat. On going out of the klavern you must remove and conceal your robe and helmet in the inner den of the klavern.

During the deliberations of the klonklave, if you wish to talk to the assembly, make a motion, or even second a motion, you must arise to your feet, then address the Exalted Cyclops by saying: **"Your Excellency,"** and touching your forehead with the ends of the fingers of your right hand. If he recognizes you, turn the palm of your right hand toward him and drop your hand, then you may speak. He will recognize you by looking at you and saying **"Klansman."** If he does not recognize you readily, then drop your hand and resume your seat, and later try again. No man will be in order unless he gets the recognition of the Exalted Cyclops by addressing him thusly.

The gavel is the emblem of authority of the Exalted Cyclops, and its signals **must** be rigidly respected. Any disrespect shown the Exalted Cyclops during a klonklave is an insult to the entire klan which he serves and an affront to our Emperor whom he represents in his official capacity. The entire klan is under direct obligations to command due respect from any and all without fear or favor.

One rap of the gavel calls for—**Silence**, and **attention**, whether you stand or sit.

45

Two raps of the gavel call for **silence and to seats.**

Three raps of the gavel call—**All to their feet.**

Remember all..........are given with the LH & A only, when B are not required.

V—S—A.
V—S—N.
S—O—G (Same is used for S—O—R).
S—O—K—C.
S—O—KLS.
S—O—F—C.
S—O—P.
A—T—S—O—P.
S—O—S.
A—T—S—O—S.
K—S.
N—H.
T—K—O—K.

THE KLONVERSATION.

*　　*　　*　　*　　*　　*　　*　　*

After the instructions have been given the Klokard will say:

"The Kladd will now conduct you to the Exalted Cyclops where you will receive from him the CS and PW, the sacred symbol, and Imperial Instructions to which give earnest heed."

The Kladd conducts the party to the station of the E. C. and says:

"Your Excellency: These klansmen (or this klansman), having been instructed in the Way of the Klavern, now awaits to receive from you the CS and PW, the sacred symbol of the klan and Imperial Instructions."

E. C. (Will arise and say): "My Fellow Klansman (or klansmen): The insignia or mark of a klansman is Honor. All secrets and secret information of the Invisible Empire is committed to you on your honor. A klansman values honor more than life itself. Be true to Honor, then to all the world you will be true.

46

Always remember that an honorable secret committed is a thing sacred.

"I am about to commit to you three vital secrets of the Invisible Empire—the CS and PW and the sacred symbol—the MIOAK. Do you swear to forever hold them in sacred, secret reverence, even unto death? _____

"The CS and PW enables you to meet with and enjoy the fellowship of klansmen in klonklave assembled.

"For the present, and until changed, the CS is_____ and the PW is _____.

"The MIOAK, the sacred symbol of the klan, is that (he explains what it is) by which klansmen recognize each other without word, sound or sign.

"I now present you with the material insignia of a klansman, the sacred symbol of the klan, by name the MIOAK. Be faithful in its wearing. It must be worn on your person where it may be readily seen. Tell no person in the whole world what it is, its meaning and significance, even by hint or insinuation, as it is a positive secret of the klan. Don't fail to recognize it by whomsoever it is worthily worn; always appreciate its sacred significance and be true to same. As a test of your honor I invest you with this symbol and commit to you its sacred secret."

He pins on the breast of the new klansman the insignia and explains its symbolic meaning.

"You will now receive Imperial Instructions. Carefully preserve and seriously study this document and give earnest heed to same, for on the practice of its teachings in your daily life depends your future advancement."

"You (or each of you) now are instructed klansmen, possessing all the rights, privileges and protection as such, will take your place with klansmen in the sacred fellowship of the Invisible Empire."

The E. C. will then give two raps with his gavel, take his seat and proceed with the other business.

47

LECTURE NO. 1.

—K-UNO—

The noble achievements of the Ku Klux Klan shine with undiminished effulgence through the gathering mist of accumulating years, an eloquent tribute to the chivalry and patriotism of the past, and the holy heroism of our fathers in preserving to us the sacred heritage of a superior race—political supremacy, racial integrity, social peace and security, and to humanity the boon of cultured civilization. It abides the malicious slanders of the age, and is an inexhaustible source of inspiration to those of this generation who aspire to all things noble and good for themselves, our country and our race.

When the shuddering peals of the thunder of the impending storm of the American Reconstruction were heard above the fading echoes of the battles of the great Civil War, the chosen victims stood aghast and pale, wondering at the meaning and purpose of the gathering gloom.

Darkness gathered apace, and the demons were loosed from hell's most dismal depths; the blighting hand of devastation complete was laid heavy upon the Southern people,—a people pauperized, bleeding, prostrated and defenseless. These noble people turned to the power of the National Government for protection but were spurned away with contempt and scorn. They had been promised protection in the possession of property, in the pursuit of peaceful employment and in every political and civil right formerly possessed by them as citizens of the national commonwealth, but the National Government, by the shameful deviltry of its unscrupulous manipulators, repudiated that solemn promise and inaugurated the most disgraceful epoch in the annals of the nations against that unarmed, defeated, defenseless and submissive people.

This great people, defenseless and friendless with a pestilence upon them more terrorizing

48

than the seven plagues of Egypt, called to the nations of the earth, but none heard their cry. That call was a horrible medley full of intense anguish,—melancholy groans and manly men struck dumb, mingling with the sickening, penetrating sobs of distressed women and the plaintive cry of hungry, cladless child; on this melancholy orchestra Grief touched the chords of universal sadness and played the direful dirge of death over the slaughtered corps of civilization.

Constitutional law was stripped by profane hands of its virtuous vestments of civilized sovereignty of four thousand years in the making, and was mocked by polluted political pirates in legislative assemblies; and by the diabolical enactments of these assemblies the hands on the dial of the clock of civilization in the tower of human progress were turned back thousands of years.

In the name of law and National Authority the property of the husband and father was ruthlessly snatched from him without provocation by the venal hand of unholy confiscation; paupers by the multitude were made in a day. Carpetbaggers, the vultures of gluttonous greed, swooped down from their aerie on the lofty peaks of the mountains of national authority o'er the dismal plain of human helplessness, fastened their tortuous talons in the fleece of defenseless innocence and consumed with avaricious avidity the vital flesh of the people's sustenance; and the scallawags—the consciencelsss, cadaverous wolves of treason—gnawed the bones remaining to a baleful state of ghastly bleaching.

The chastity of the mother, wife, sister and daughter was imperiled and their sacred persons were placed in jeopardy to the licentious longings of lust-crazed beasts in human form. Might ruled over Right. Life and living was made intolerable; the rasping, discordant notes of penury had displaced the heavenly harmony of domestic happiness and no man's home was secure.

Ignorance, Lust and Hate seized the reins of State, and riot, rapine and universal ruin reigned supreme; the highest form of cultured society was thrust down and its noble neck was forced under the iron heel of pernicious passion who yielded a potent scepter of inquisitorial oppression, and the very blood of the Caucasian race was seriously threatened with an everlasting contamination.

That anguish-laden cry of that defenseless people of the Southland, was heard and answered by the gallant knights of the Invisible Empire, and not one faltered or failed as Duty pointed the way in the cause of humanity and civilization; with a grim smile of sacred duty resting upon their manly countenances, impelled by an instinct of the race, they leaped into the saddle, borne upon the back of their faithful steeds, baptized with a suffusion of tears, they came; they came, they saw, they conquered! From over the mysterious borderland from the Empire of the Soul the Ku Klux came. They were knight errantry in the highest, noblest and gravest form personified. They responded to that call a hundred thousand strong, and rode forth with no blast of the trumpet or cheering shouts of the populace; without the inspiration of oral eloquence or stirring strains of martial music, they rode forth to brave dangers and hardships unknown and to face death in a thousand forms.

They dissipated the cruel storm of the American reconstruction and won the plaudits of an intelligent, unprejudiced world. They stemmed the murky tide of despotic usurpation and tyrannical greed, and rescued the entire country from utter disgrace and ruin. They re-established racial rights and the sovereignty of constitutional law, redressed the wrong, made secure political supremacy, started anew the wheels of industry and made possible the birth of the greatest nation of all time—the Re-United States of America.

With a "fiery cross", symbol of the purest

and most loyal patriotism, as their beacon, the Ku Klux rode through the darkness of Reconstruction's night; they dispelled the dense darkness of that frightful night, and at the rising of the sun of a glorious day, they saw the shades of that awful night receding. Right had been by them established over Might. The voice of music was again heard in the land; their purpose and mission was ended; they laid aside their spotless robes, and the greatest order of chivalry in all history disbanded—for the Ku Klux rode no more.

The noble ride of the Ku Klux Klan is immortalized by their accomplishments, and is memorialized by the men of today who appreciate the chilvaric, holy and patriotic achievements of the original Klan in the permanence of this our great fraternity.

The Spirit of the Ku Klux Klan still lives, and should live a priceless heritage to be sacredly treasured by all those who love their country, regardless of section, and are proud of its sacred traditions. That this spirit may live always to warm the hearts of manly men, unify them by the spirit of holy clanishness, to assuage the billowing tide of fraternal alienation that surges in human breasts, and inspire them to achieve the highest and noblest in the defense of our country, our homes, each other and humanity, is the paramount ideal of the Knights of the Ku Klux Klan.

When the baleful blast of Reconstruction's
     storm was o'er,
The valiant, chivalric Ku Klux rode no more.
But ride on and on, thou spirit of that mystic
     klan,
In your noble mission for humanity's good;
Until the clanish tie of klancraft binds man to
     man
For our country, our homes and womanhood.

"Non Silba Sed Anthar."

All say in unison—"Not for self but for others."

KNIGHTS OF THE KU KLUX KLAN
TITLES AND EXPLANATIONS

THE INVISIBLE EMPIRE—Geographically the universal jurisdiction of the order.

A REALM—A sub-division of the Invisible Empire—a state or territory of the United States.

A PROVINCE—A sub-division of a Realm—a county or a number of counties of a State or Territory.

A KLANTON—The jurisdiction of a klan, from **Canton**—a corner or a small district.

THE IMPERIAL KLONVOKATION—Is the Convention of the Invisible Empire and is the supreme legislative body of the Order, —from **convocation**—an assembly called by higher authority.

A KLORERO—Is the convention of a Realm from **Korero**—a convention.

A KLONVERSE—Is the assembly of a Province, from **converse**—as in a conversation or conference.

A KLONKLAVE—Is the gathering in secret session of a klan, from **conclave**—a secret meeting or locked room.

THE GOVERNMENT of the Invisible Empire is vested with the Imperial Wizard, the Emperor, assisted by his fifteen Genii—the Imperial Officers constituting his official family; the government of a Realm is vested with a Grand Dragon, assisted by his nine Hydras—the Grand Officers; the government of a Province is vested with a Great Titan, assisted by his twelve Furies—the Great Officers, and a Klan is governed by an Exalted Cyclops, assisted by his twelve Terrors —the elective officers of a klan.

THE KLORAN (The Book of the Klan)— Ritual and Lectures.

52

KLAVERN—The meeting place of a klan; from **cavera**—a large cave.

KLAN—The unit of the Order; from **clan**—a number of men of kindred purpose who are bound together by an oath and who are very determined to enhance and protect each other's interest and welfare.

KLANSMAN—A member of the klan; the title of the first Order, or K-Uno.

KLAN KOURIER—The title of the Official Organ.

KLAVALIER—The soldier of the klan (Military Department), from **cavalier**—a courtly, polite, cultured and very courageous and skilful soldier of the 17th and 18th century.

KLAVALKADE—A parade or other public exhibition; from **cavalcade**—a procession.

ANNO KLAN—In the year of the Klan; written thus: AK.

ANNO DOMINI—In the year of our Lord; written thus: AD.

IMPERIAL WIZARD—The Emperor of the Invisible Empire; a wise man; a wonder-worker, having power to charm and control, from **Vita**—to know. The title is taken from the chief officer of the original Ku Klux Klan, who was designated as the Grand Wizard.

KLALIFF—A successor in office.

KLOKARD—Lecturer or Teacher of the Klan, from **Klo** of Kloran, the book, and **Kard**, meaning a teacher or reader.

KLUDD—Chaplain, from **Culdee**—the high priest of the ancient Druids.

KLIGRAPP—The Secretary, from **Kirogra-**pher—one whose business is to write.

KLABEE—The Treasurer, from **Kaba**—to keep, and **Kees**, an ancient Egyptian coin and means a purse.

KLADD—The Conductor, from **Kada**—to lead or pull.

KLAROGO—The Inner Guard, from **caveo**—to stop or beware, and **interrogate**, to question.

KLEXTER—The Outer Guard, from **Ken**—to look all around with the eyes, and **External**—outside.

KLOKAN—An Investigator, from **Ko'**—to know, and **Kannas**—with the eyes.

KLOKANN—The plural of Klokan—The Board of Investigators and Advisers.

IMPERIAL KLONCILIUM—The Supreme Executive Committee; composed of all the Imperial Officers.

IMPERIAL KLEPEER—A Supreme Delegate, from the words **delegate** and **peers**.

GRAND DRAGON—A title from the original Ku Klux Klan—the Chief Officer of a Realm.

GREAT TITAN—A title from the original Ku Klux Klan—the Chief Officer of a Province.

EXALTED CYCLOPS—The Chief Officer of a klan. Cyclops is from the original Ku Klux Klan.

KLEAGLE—Title of an Organizer for the Order.

GIANT—A title from the original Ku Klux Klan. A Klan Giant is a Past Exalted Cyclops; a Great Giant is a Past Great Titan; a Grand Giant is a Past Grand Dragon; an Imperial Giant is a Past Imperial Wizard.

NIGHT-HAWK—A title from the original Ku Klux Klan. He is the custodian of the Fiery Cross, which he carries in all ceremonies and Klavalkades. He entertains waiting aliens just prior to their naturalization.

www.ingramcontent.com/pod-product-compliance
Lightning Source LLC
Chambersburg PA
CBHW081115280526
45787CB00007B/2838